...always believe in the natural power and wisdom of the American native people...

This book is dedicated to all those who actively or passively participated in its creation in any way!

And the following people I would thank by name:

Elizabeth Winker	Germany / South Dakota
John Winker	St. Paul, Minnesota
Pat Winker	Howard, South Dakota
Dan Winker	Minneapolis, Minnesota
Jerry Winker	Howard, South Dakota
Nancy Winker	Sioux Falls, South Dakota
Harold Winker	Howard, South Dakota
Christina Winker	Howard, South Dakota
Paul Winker	Howard, South Dakota
Samantha Winker	Howard, South Dakota
Clara Winker	Howard, South Dakota
Barney Wagner, Sr.	Platte, South Dakota
Connie Wagner	Platte, South Dakota
Barney Wagner, Jr.	Sturgis, South Dakota
Connie Wagner	Sturgis, South Dakota
Richard Wagner (Dick)	Dimmock, South Dakota
Marsha Wagner	Dimmock, South Dakota
Neil Burghardt	Brookings, South Dakota
Benjamin Katona	Rastatt, Germany

Lothar R. Schulz

Our Cool Run to Sturgis 2017

Trip on a Damned Endless Highway Through South Dakota

Bibliographic information from the German National Library:
The German National Library lists this publication in the German National Library;
Detailed bibliographic data are available on the Internet at http://dnb.dnb.de.

Illustration: **Lou** (Lothar R. Schulz)
Further Contributors: **Liz** (Elizabeth A. Winker)

Production and publishing: BoD – Books on Demand, Norderstedt
ISBN: 978-3-7460-6174-0

Preface

This account of my journey is designed in the form of a diary, which should mainly tell the story though the many and sometimes striking images. Pretty much everything that seemed interesting in any way was recorded. Therefore, you should not be surprised if you see and read things here that also serve as memories for the author. But perhaps it just this characteristic that distinguishes this "work" from other books in a hopefully quite pleasant way ...!

This book should not only convey information about the actual experience; most importantly, it should also reflect some of what was perceived and experienced through subjective impressions in the most diverse situations. You, the reader, or should I say the viewer of the pictures, are invited to join me as intensively as possible in my itinerary. I hope you can absorb some of the magic and energy as we take our road trip across some of the highways through the US-Midwest, the American prairie, and to our ultimate destination – the world's largest motorcycle party, "STURGIS", in the State of South Dakota (SD) and surrounding area.
You are invited to get a little taste of the passion and enjoyment of this journey through this still rough and untamed country, and maybe also get an appetite for what maybe – if at all – possible to express with black letters on white paper.

The journey's motto from the beginning was:

The path is the goal, or...:

... LET IT GO WITH THE FLOW ... !

You are welcome to enjoy...!!!

Our journey began on July 26th, 2107, in Karlsruhe and ended on August 16th, 2017, at the same place. We flew with Lufthansa from Frankfurt/M via Chicago and then on to Minneapolis, Minnesota, and for a price of about 800 Euros, it proved to be quite affordable. (Flying the next day would have been about 500 Euros more due to the summer holiday season).

July 26th(Wednesday)
Upon arrival in Minneapolis, we were picked up by John Winker, who lives very close to St. Paul. The jet lag took over quite quickly, and so after a few welcoming beers at 2 o'clock in the morning (local time), we were really exhausted, and so we fell into bed with a smile as we drifted deep into the realm of dreams ...

John Winker's ,68 Ford Falcon in front of his house in St. Paul.

…because we had arrived now, at the starting point of our trip, which was to lead us through the expanses of the American Midwest. In a part of the country where the clocks run differently, and the rhythm of life differs from ours in a subtle as well as decisive way.

You can get used to it quickly, very quickly ...

July 27th (Thursday)

After about 5 hours of sleep, we are awakened by the sirens of a remote police car or ambulance. A sound reminding me of pleasant memories of exciting American films from my childhood and youth.

Yes, we are here now, in the land of unlimited possibilities.

By the way, John's place in Juno Avenue is only about 4 miles from where the "colored" Philandro Castiles was "accidentally" killed in a vehicle check last year on July 6, 2016. He was shot 7 times by a police officer as he went to pull out his driver's license out of his back pocket. (The case went through the press). Incidentally, Philandro was stopped only because of a defective brake light on his car. The policeman was acquitted in spite of the quite clear situation and citizen protests. The only consequence was that he was removed from the police force as ...

US – also a land of "impossible" opportunities ...

> **SO IF GUNS KILL PEOPLE, I GUESS PENCILS MISS SPELL WORDS, CARS DRIVE DRUNK AND SPOONS MAKE PEOPLE FAT.**

But we are in "luck", since none of us are "colored" and we have made sure that all of the taillights are working on the bikes, so we do not have to be concerned ...

Because ... shit happens every day ... and everywhere !

THE BIKE: The Victory (V92C, BJ 1999, ID No. 379) is a convincingly powerful 1500cc engine with 58hp and has just over 14,000 miles on the odometer. It is one of the first machines of this brand, and spent many as an exhibit in the showroom of a retailer in Minnesota. John purchased it last October for this trip, and got it for about $4500. The sound of its engine roars and bubbles with its open tailpipes, penetrating hard, similar to a Harley, but somehow biting and therefore very impressive!

Photo from left to right: Karin Winker (Dan Winker's wife), Elizabeth Winker, Dan Winker (John und Elizabeth's brother) und John Winker

Caption: John's garage in St. Paul with both motorcycles (Victory V92C und
Honda Valkyrie, with its6 cylinder boxer-motor…Turbine sound)

For my first trip with this bike, we took the adjacent freeway and I was without a helmet, which by the way, is not compulsory here. We went to a motorcycle dealer where I got one though. So now with my helmet, I am comfortable, used to cruising as in good old Germany ...

... because in my adolescent age of 50 years, one should be somewhat reasonable, although perhaps only in the approach ... and I do not want to do what is done here by most with such incredible care freeness (about 90% of bikers ride here without a helmet!).

After that stop, we wanted to visit a friendly Indian dealer, a half-Indian, but he was in Las Vegas on business ...

We drove there in John's "new" black 1968 Ford Falcon, which he recently purchased for $1500 and has already restored at least so it is ready to drive. The old-timer squeaks and rattles from front to back, the suspension vibrates like a rolling ship in the high seas when accelerating and braking, but it's just great fun to roll over the highways while the car radio plays cool sounds of current underground music I do not know from home, so ...

John on the left and me (Lou) on the right waiting on the parking lot at the Indian dealer

It's a relaxed and fun activity on this first day.

It's rumored that John's great-grandmother on the maternal side was likely an Indian (Sioux or Cheyenne), and maybe that is one of the reasons why everything is down to earth and very familiar and friendly.

Another small highlight for me was the revolver John had inherited from his father. It's a magnum 44 "Dirty Harry". With this weapon, you could kill a grizzly bear with only one shot. You should note though that firing should only be done two-handed and with a firm grip, as the kick is absolutely brutal! Even some experienced shooters want to leave this weapon alone...

Here in Minnesota, as well as in South Dakota, almost everyone has one or more firearms, because it just sounds good, and it's about as normal as when we Germans carry a pocket knife in trousers.

…and here I could not resist getting photographed with this rare and notorious weapon ...

In the evening, we went to eat pizza with John's siblings and walked by a liquor store...

In some states, alcoholic beverages may only be sold in such liquor stores. In the 70's, there was also the possibility to buy drinks via the "Drive-Through Liquor Store". A 21-year-old driver was allowed to buy this way, but not the passenger. In addition, alcohol may not be transported inside the car, but only in the trunk.

Alcohol prices are at least half the price higher than in Germany. For a small 6-pack of beer, you pay around $8-14, for example ...

A 0.7-liter bottle of "Jack Daniels Fire" costs $23 (in Germany €18)

Other countries, … other manners!

July 28th (Friday)
Today we drove around in St. Paul and Minneapolis, browsing various shops, shopping, eating out and getting the bikes ready for the tour ...

So a normal day, with a few impressions on the way ...!

Photos taken in an outdoor store in Minnesota

No comment: ... or:

USA is a heaven for real weapon fans/fools and those who want to be one!

When shopping, you should always make sure that you take as big of shopping cart as possible into the store ...!

PS: Weapons of all calibers can be bought quite cheaply in pawnshops, if they are not picked up in time by the owner after expiration of the redemption period ...By the way, there are pawn shops in almost every neighborhood.

The gun laws are quite lax here. After an official background check, which takes about 24 hours, "respectable" citizens can buy an almost unlimited numbers of weapons and ammunition ...

The day is drawing to a close and we are on the way back in the '68 Falcon ...
It's Friday night and next Monday we are finally off to the west, in the direction of the mega-party, to the Mecca of all thoroughbred bikers, and we want to ride on less-frequented highways.

Whenever possible, we will avoid freeways and interstates, where it is perfectly normal to get passed on the left or on the right by big trucks going 70 - 85 miles per hour (110 – 140km/h), and therefore leaving powerful air turbulences behind to make the biker struggle.

We also do not need to get there quickly, but instead want to have an enjoyable, relaxed joyride, meet a few people on the way, and visit interesting places.

The route planning is over, the countdown is on, we are curious, and relax a little while with a cool "Colt 45" malt beer in the evening sun ...

July 29th, 2017(Saturday)

The day starts with plenty of coffee and some American chocolate cookies., after which we took a trip to Nelson across the state border to Wisconsin to eat a deliciously juicy big burger at a cool biker pub.

The bikers ride here almost all on extremely crazy bikes, each more beautiful and violent than the other, and helmets are shunned as the devil does holy water. Here, nobody wants anyone to tell them how to behave. Sunglasses and bandanas are the rule when riding these fat blubbering machines. There is an atmosphere of freedom, adventure, serenity and enjoyment. The American bikers know what is important.

I'm convinced and inspired ...!

Because real fun always has a taste of unchained and hot spice ...

What is striking here compared to Germany is that you frequently see an American flag hanging on people's houses. The Americans are a proud people. In particular, the immigrants of the last few decades express their gratitude for finding a chance for a better life here ...

July 30th, 2017(Sunday)

... on the way to breakfast at about 10:30 in the '68 Falcon ...

... last briefing before leaving the next day, heading "WEST" ...

July 31st, 2017(Monday)

Today things get serious. Our trip out West starts now, leaving St. Paul towards the South...

The journey from St. Paul to Howard is about 260 miles or 420km that we will tackle today. Excitement is paired with a feeling of uncertainty ...

We start the ride, I'm on the Victory, John is on his Honda Valkyrie, and Elizabeth (Liz) is driving the Ford Falcon with all the luggage. We leave shortly after 10 o'clock in the morning. Every 60-70 miles we have scheduled breaks to stretch and/or refuel our vehicles. There were only a few clouds in the sky and the temperatures were around 29°C (84°F). The bikes as well as the Ford Falcon run perfectly. It seemed like a pretty easy trip. Only 14 days ago, the weather forecast claimed it would be warm – yes, very warm. For the period from late July to mid-August, temperatures around Sturgis as well as throughout South Dakota were predicted to be between 35 and 41°C (95 and 106°F), and that it would feel like 43-44°C (110 – 112°F) in the shade. When I heard this, I considered throwing in the whole trip because I did not want to be cooked on the road, especially here where there are no shadows to hide under. On the route there are sometimes narrow telephone poles and sometimes a store, a farmhouse, or a gas station, but even these only provide thin shadows at high noon.

But fortunately the forecast was not correct, and the weather could not have been better, it was as if we had ordered it. A weather for angels, for both good and bad, that's the way it should be!

… ABSOLUTELY PERFECT!!!

After about 30 miles of driving, and while we were still in quite heavy traffic in the more populated area of St. Paul/Minneapolis, with quite a few construction zones on Highway13, we took a short side trip and were almost separated from each other. John had turned left with his motorcycle on a busy highway fork in the middle of a construction zone, and I and Liz with the Falcon kept going straight because we had just lost sight of him. However, we saw John standing on the median directly after the fork on the other side waiting for us so we could correct the error by driving carefully crossing the median to get to the other lane.

The traffic on Highway13 slowly eased up as we headed towards Jordan, and so were getting more and more the feeling of "easy riding", as you know it from the movies of the 60s and 70s.

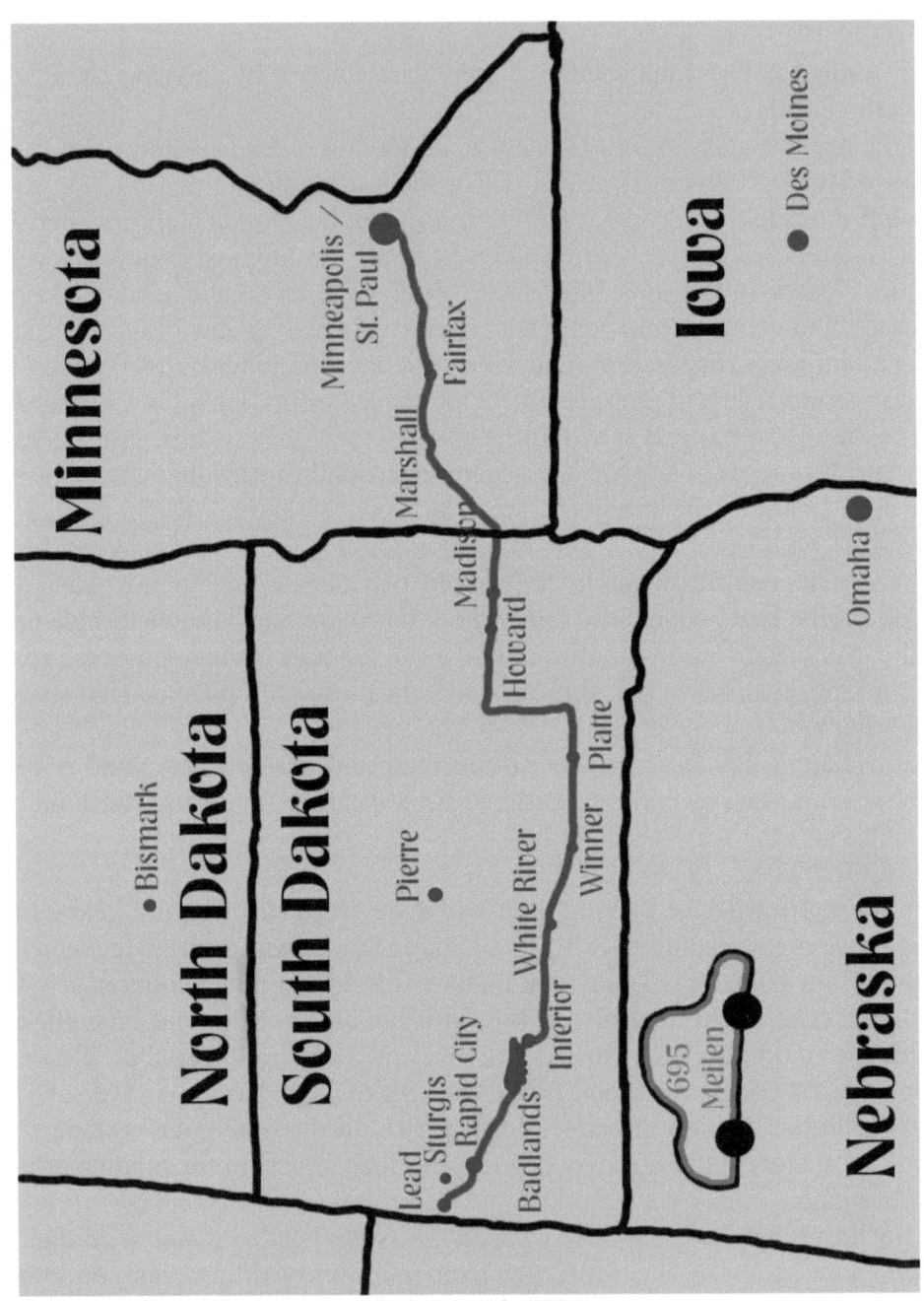

Our route from St. Paul (MN) to Sturgis (SD)

In Jordan, we stopped and got beef jerky and coffee at the gas station. Our second stop was at Fairfax (HYW44), the third in Marshall and again in Madison where we stocked ourselves in a liquor store with beer. At the stop in Marshall, we laid down in a park-like area near the local golf course for about a half an hour in the freshly cut grass and in the shade of a tree to relax a bit and recharge our batteries for the tired bones.

When we got up, John could not find the key to his Honda anymore.
Oh no, if we do not find the key now, we have a small problem because of the absence of a replacement key. John has one, but it was about 165 miles east in St. Paul ...After a short but intense search, we found it, but probably only because the height of the grass was luckily quite low!

About half an hour later we crossed the State Border from the East and entered South Dakota (SD).

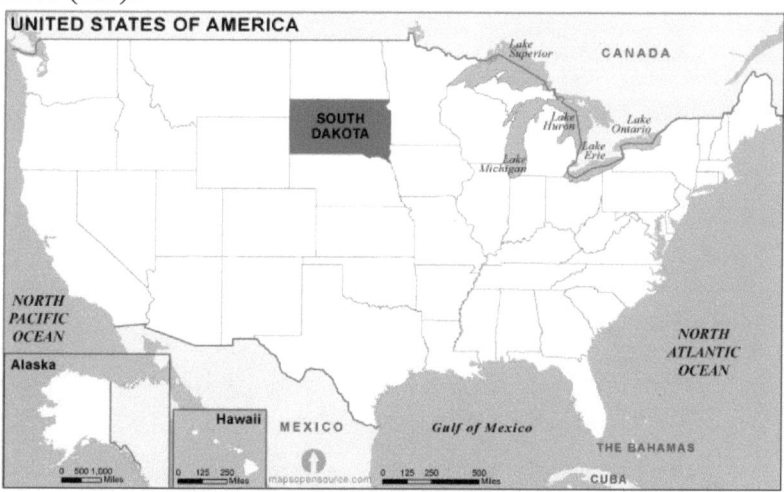

Quelle: Maps Open Source, http://www.mapsopensource.com/south-dakota-location-map.html
Lizenz: Creative Commons Attribution 3.0 Unported License.

SD is located in the northern part of the Midwest of America.
Only about 850,000 people live here, although it is 60% of Germany's size. More wildlife than humans are at home here, which makes it a paradise for nature lovers as well as hunters.
Here you can still quite clearly feel the spirit of the "Wild West" ...!

At about 8 pm, we arrived at our motel in Howard. The first longer jaunt was behind us; we were already a lot closer to our goal ... but the real experience was, of course, the journey to get there ...

In the gas station next to our motel, which is right at the entrance to the town, I was able to get a bottle of "Jack Daniels Fire" to celebrate the first day/part of the trip and so relished the taste as it went down my throat!

Here are a few impressions on the way ... at the gas station in Fairfax

…short break after filling up in Fairfax

…it`s better to give the old car a short look before starting again…!

…on the highway near Madison, rush hour in South Dakota (SD) 😊

Arrival ... in the evening in front of the motel in Howard, SD

August 1st, 2017 (Tuesday)

The motel is right next to a gas station on Highway 34, where occasionally heavy trucks drive through, and currently also a relatively large number of bikers on their Harleys in small groups or alone, but mainly driving in the direction of the West ... the ultimate meeting of the year ...!

Instead of carrying passengers, the machines are heavily packed, and most of the baggage is strapped securely to the sissy bar.

You can feel it in the air; the tension is slowly but noticeably increasing. This image of bikers, almost all without any protective clothing, is something that can only be described as a procession of freedom-loving nomads. I have never seen anything in this kind and dimension in Germany. Whether it is related to the vastness of the country or the type of American pioneer who loves challenges and adventure ... no idea ...

Nobody is in a hurry, and you do not see any Japanese sports machines or foreign sports cars ...

We are here in South Dakota (SD), which is about 60% of the size of Germany, but where only about 850,000 people live.

(in Germany there are about 82 million) ...

Part of this day's program was a visit to see John and Liz's mother in Howard, and have an evening barbecue.

We also visited her brother Jerry, who lives on a farm a bit out of the woods with his four children. He is a keen and responsible gun lover who has rifles, pistols and revolvers of all calibers in showcases and suitcases and bags all over the house, and he also sometimes makes his own ammunition.

After an interesting conversation, he invited us to return after the Sturgis Rally to shoot together.

I'm looking forward to shooting with his AK 47 (Kalashnikov), a special version for paratroopers, which he has in his pick-up, and one or the other shotgun or revolver ...

But more about this later ...

This picture is dedicated to Patty, John and Liz's Mom, taken in her yard, and which deserves a very special place of honor in this book.

She welcomed us very hospitably, provided us with good food and drinks, and always had an open ear for us.

Here I was also able to meet John and Liz's other 4 siblings, all of whom are very interesting and friendly, each in his or her own way.

We all enjoyed this time together in Howard, SD, and we gladly remember it.

Patty also has a key to the museum in Howard, where we found some surprising things when we visited it on our return trip from Sturgis...

But more about that later ...☺

August 2nd, 2017(Wednesday)

As always, we started the day easy, and were invited John and Liz's Mom (Patty) for a hearty omelet breakfast. Then I was able to type a few lines and download a few images for the manuscript of this book, to make sure that I am able to bring everything to "paper" while it is still relatively fresh...

Our support vehicle for luggage and possible emergencies, the '68 Ford Falcon, we exchanged with brother Jerry's 2010 Ford Flex, because the Flex has better brakes, power steering, air conditioning ... etc.

The main road going through Howard (Highway34) showing the town's huge grain silo! You see such silos here on the average about every 30-40 miles. The farmers deliver their grain at such silos, where it then typically market in the form of Cooperation.

This afternoon we will drive to Platte (about 115 miles, 184km) to visit an uncle. This is more or less on the way to Sturgis and leads us through a scenic area.

After refueling and taking a small break, we noticed that a big stain has formed under the Victory...

What on earth was that?

Fortunately, it was only the overflow from the gas tank, where gas was able to spill out because of the tilt of the bike on the side stand ...

The ride could start now ...

We passed endlessly large corn and soybean fields, and the smells changed frequently from pig manure in the fields, or the light and fine scent of the plants growing in the fields, and in places also the smell of decay from the smaller or larger flattened animals (raccoons, deer, deer, big geese, and other smaller birds) lying on or next to the road, referred to as "roadkill" here. If you run over a skunk here, you can smell the stinging stench of its defense gland for weeks.

The sky slowly darkened more and more, and about 20 miles before Platte, it began to rain heavily and the view as well as the fun-factor dropped quite quickly down to "ZERO". John, who rode ahead with his bike, had to stop because of the spray mist from an oncoming truck, which, in a fraction of a second, fogged up his motorcycle glasses from the inside. He had to stop dry them out because he could not see anything at all.

But after another 7 miles, we made it to Platte and also found Uncle Barney's house, in which we could dry and warm up with a good beer and delicious barbecued chicken.

Uncle Barney, with his 77 years, is a really cool and fun companion. He told us that he upgraded his Harley's 106 engine to replace it with a Screaming Eagle 110cubic inch one. Once it hits about 140 mph (about 220km/h), it's a bit too fast for him ... ☺

He spends his time buying houses, renovating them, and selling them again. Just last year, he retired and came back to SD from Arizona with his wife, Connie. Now he is currently working on another home construction project where he will be in charge of doing the electrical and plumbing work. The house in which he currently lives is also being refurnished by him to then sell again for a higher price after they move to the new house.

He used to be a Production Manager in a furniture factory in an Indian reservation. Since the Native Americans did not show any discipline and punctuality there, and did not really want to learn them, this project was condemned to failure after a relatively short time. The Native Americans often came to work only when they needed money, and when they thought it was enough, they just didn't come back. The Native Americans get a kind of basic security from the American government since they live on reservations and have been made to renounce large parts of their land. This basic security, coupled with the loss of tradition, identity and dignity, causes many families to slip into alienation and resignation and then turn to alcohol where they decline and sink into poverty. But even one of Barney's ancestors may have been a Native American, but that's another story ... After some interesting stories from his life and good drinks, it was time for us to go to bed. We will spend the night here to ride another 350 miles (about 540km) early the next morning to our "cabin" at "Terry Peak" in the Black Hills ..

August 3rd, 2017(Thursday)

Departure is at 8:15, across the Missouri River to Winner, White River, Interior (Cowboy Corner), through the Badlands to Wall and back through the Badlands to Rapid City, and then via Deadwood to Lead to our cabin at Terry Peak.

The rain had stopped that morning, and the clothes could be dried overnight with a warm-air blower, but the sky was still very gray and not inviting to continue. Still – he who has a clear goal and two travel companions should not hesitate just because not the sun is not shining. We rode off and I sensed quite quickly that the low temperatures and yesterday's ride in the rain had left its mark on me.

During the short stop at the Missouri River, I dug out one of the sweatshirts that John's mother gave us as a precaution and put it on. I now felt a little better, but also noticed that if it did not get warmer soon, I would probably catch a cold.

…just before crossing the Missouri River, still on the east side!

We enter the western part of the state, which is not as green as in the East ...

On the west side, we have to adjust our clocks, which we're not wearing by the way, by an hour (Rocky-Mountain-Time).

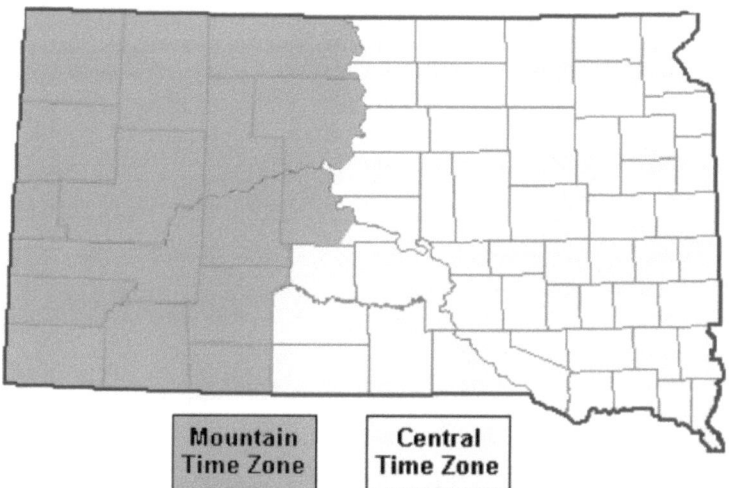

Quelle: TimeTemperature.com http://www.timetemperature.com/tzmaps/sdtz.gif

At the next stop in "Winner", we were in the store next to a gas station to warm up with a hot coffee, strengthen ourselves with Beef Jerky, and go to the bathroom again. Liz and John were startled as they looked into my glassy eyes and recognized my slight drowsiness caused by the weakening of the approaching cold. I told them that I did not feel well and hoped that the weather would soon be better. After a 20-minute break, and as we rode further to the west, the temperatures dropped to about 13-14° C (55-57°F) and it even began to drizzle slightly. But after about a half an hour, it became drier and the horizon gradually brightened, and the temperatures rose slightly.
I felt relief and my discomfort and weakness gave way to a better and more stable feeling of recovery.

The next stop to refuel was in White River, where we refueled ourselves with enough coffee from paper cups and chatted with a few bikers, all of whom were on their way to Sturgis. The bikers here are different than in Europe, most are really cool, in a good mood, and happy to have a quick and easy conversation. When they found out that I am from Germany, they were always kind-hearted and wished us a "good ride" with a raised thumb and a smile.

About half of the way to Sturgis was behind us and the weather and the temperatures were luckily more pleasant!

Shortly after the refueling stop in White River, a medium-sized dog ran across the street in front of us. An emergency stop prevented worse, because the timing would have been just right to make John and I have to jump off the bikes. In contrast to us, this black-and-white spotted stray dog's pulse didn't likely speed up even just a bit.

He just wanted to run across the street at that exact point in time, which he did about 1-2 meters in front of us, and with a slightly irritated look. The same thing would happen to us twice with antelopes near the Badlands, which also decided to change the side of the road just in front of us.

"Cowboy Corner" gas station in Interior, very close to the Badlands. More and more bikers are appearing at the gas stations; they all know only one direction ...STURGIS (SD)...!

Snapshots in the gas station "Cowboy Corner" in Interior…

… the ride and the versatile impressions is what makes it meaningful …!From the gas station, you can already recognize the Badlands from afar.

... and the winding roads in the wasteland are very attractive in their own way !

Drive through the Badlands to Wall with stop over…

... right in the middle of the lunar landscape; you just have to let it sink in!

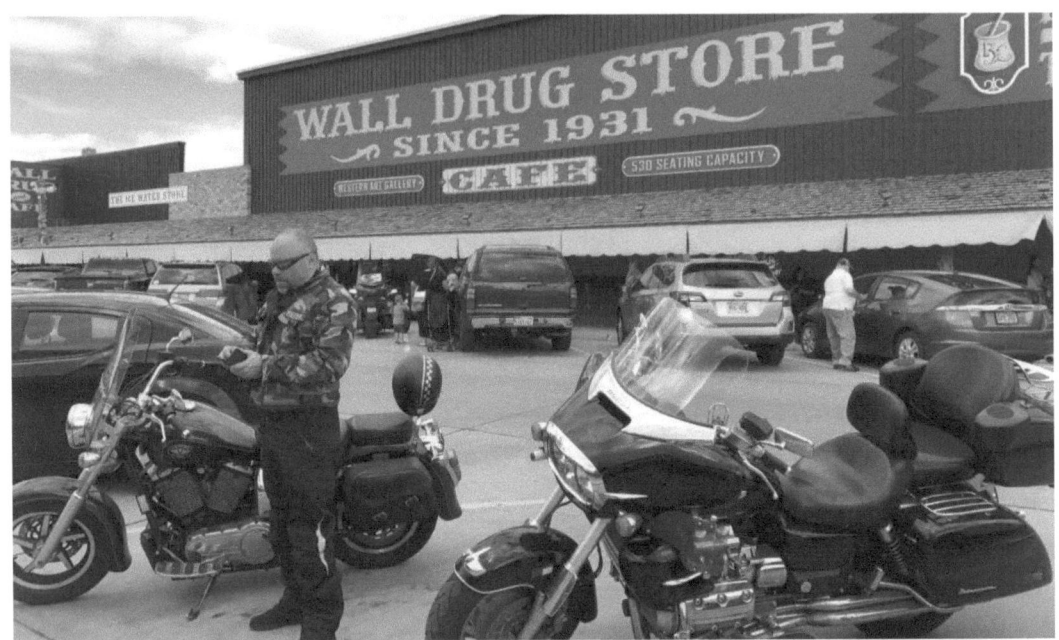

Wall, there were real Buffalo burgers with well-hopped beer to strengthen us

A "Jackolope" in a store in Wall (rabbit with antlers and chicken feet)

Ride on a gravel road...
We took the shortcut, as it was already quite late and we wanted to reach our cabin before dark.

When we arrived at our cabin Lead/Deadwood at about 8:30 pm, it was only 47° F (about 8° C) and I had no problem with quickly lighting the fire in the wood stove to warm us up. The day had gone very well and we had put 349 miles (about 560 km) behind us.

Arrival at the cabin at Terry Peak (terrace in the back)
→ 5 nights for a total of $1800.00 (main season/Bikeweek)

The best beer is the ice cold one you drink after a hard day while relaxing in a "hot" Jacuzzi tub behind the wooden cabin !!!

The cabin is also spacious and very cozy on the inside…

John in front of his Honda Valkyrie and me next to the Victory at the cabin in Lead (Deadwood) at Terry Peak at about 2000m above sea level.

August 4th, 2017(Friday)
Spearfish Canyon (similar to the Black Forest) with long curves + wide roads, a short trip in the afternoon to Main Street in Sturgis & Buffalo Chip!

August 5th, 2017(Saturday)

On this Saturday, the weather wasn't so good so we decided to visit Devil's Tower in Wyoming (16°F/61°F and rain on the return journey). In the evening, we went to the FIREHOUSE (brewery in a former fire station) in Rapid City and checked out the local beer brewed there.

Driving the Ford Flex through the Black Hills to Wyoming

…Bikers we met on the way…

Devils Tower from afar (264m high, a Native American sanctuary)

Devils Tower at a closer proximity…

Among other things, Elizabeth Winker, is also a good Native American (Style) flute player ...!

Longhorn cattle near Devil's Tower …

Wild buffalo near Devil's Tower ...

…Bikers we met on the way…!

One of many bikes at the Devil's Tower parking lot…

Return from Wyoming to Deadwood/Lead on Interstate-90

Native American art ... in a store in Rapid City

...try to get him... fleeing the cop - Indian on an Indian ...! ☺

In the "Firehouse" (brewery/restaurant) in Rapid City ...

…and awesome bikes again, in front of the Firehouse, and they are very loud!

… and the beer tasted good…

… very good, … almost too good!!! ☺ ☺

August 6th, 2017(Sunday)

This morning, the wide and long curves of the Nemo Road were the plan ... and they really are a poem, charming nature with rugged cliffs beside lush trees, and most of all, many bikers who want the same thing, gliding along the road and take the curves with "steam" wherever and whenever they come.

At lunchtime we were in Sturgis and mingled with the bikers, "lost" ourselves and thoroughly enjoyed it ...

Hell had broken loose on Main Street of the 7000-person town. Harleys as far as the eye can see. In four rows, the iron heaps from Milwaukee park: bike to bike on both sides of the road, in the middle, they are parked headlights on headlights. The narrow lanes in-between serve as a boulevard. "Blubber, blubber" - the machines saunter up and down the street, each as unique as their rider: Tourers bristling with chrome, stretched Dynas, widened Fat Boys, minimalistic Sportster, some built beyond recognition where only the V2 engine gives it away that it's a Harley. Riders are fat, thin, bearded, bald, tattooed and shaved - men and women who at first glance, in addition to the passion for Harleys, are united by their intense sunburns.

On the side streets, there are the policemen who are recruited from all over the US, since Sturgis itself only has its own 15 cops. First and foremost, they regulate the traffic, making sure that the stalking monster mopeds really stop at the stop signs. Regarding the machines, the law enforcement officers show at most private interest –in official business, they have nothing to complain about.

Allowed is what pleases - and what sounds good. Here the bikes don't need to have front brakes and can have empty exhaust stubs. Muffler in the exhausts? Officer Luke U laughs: "They're really required in Germany? Man, we're a free country here" he says, switching on his neon-blue engine lights. The only important rule for bikers in South Dakota: Anyone who rides without a helmet – and everyone is allowed to and does from the age of 18 - must wear glasses to protect their eyes. Otherwise, sparse clothing is part of the program, the specifications here: panties and hidden nipples. At least during the day, most of them stick to it.

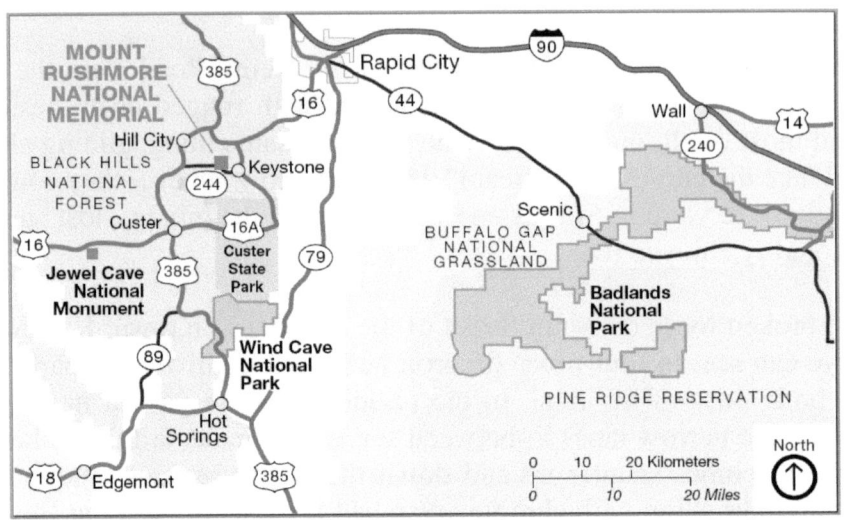

On the following pages, you find impressions of the hustle and bustle on Main Street in Sturgis and surroundings ...,

… because pictures tell much more than 1000 of words…!

Yesssssssss !!!

STURGIS … the „real" PARTY!!!

Main Street in Sturgis… the air is burning of tension and pleasure!

…Bikes, Bikes…

…and again Bikesss…!

Main Street and all surrounding streets were almost completely full with parked bikes.

Everyone basically only does what they like ... what else? !!!
... and the police hold back ...

See and be seen... the show is going on...

...sharp and blatant!

Hardly a moment without fascinating impressions ...!

... everybody joins in, none is left out in the cold ...

Had enough to drink; go quickly back to the "smurf village" ...

…and always in the mood for more ...!

Naked skin is often quickly painted and presented ...

…everything is cool…!

Sturgis was not always like this

Eighty years ago, Sturgis was an unknown and backward town on the edge of Highway 34, in which the glorious past was the paramount talk of the town. Located just north of Deadwood, Sturgis was founded in the 1850s by people in search of gold, who hoped for a quick fortune. Miners, dreamers, and bar ladies/dancers used to live here, hoping for the luck of the yellow ore coming from the mines around the Black Hills.

Many of them died during the cruel cold winters, some of them falling victim to the arrows or axes of the Indians - Arapahoes, Black-footed Indians, Cheyenne and Sioux - provoked by the invasion of the white man in their holy homeland. Others died as they lived, in dire poverty, sickness and misery, their hopes and dreams shattered on the ground of reality. Only the strong, or those who were very lucky, survived. Men like the legendary Bill Hickok, gunfighter and card player who was killed by a bullet from a stranger in poker game. These were men who lived for the moment, who had worked hard and/or played hard. They often put everything on one single card. No wonder they were hated by the Indians, these lawless raiders from the cities of the East, men who were driven by weapons and especially greed. But gold attracts such daring courageous lucky knights, and the greed for more and more led these men also to extraordinary achievements. Life was hard and the men harder. They had to be like that because they had little choice. But that's all very long ago and the gold rush has long been history ...

Ironically, it was just this lonely seclusion of the Black Hills settlements that soon made the name Sturgis famous again. JC "Pappy" Hotel, or just Pappy as his friends called him, was more than bored with the situation at the time. He was tired of wasting his life waiting, hoping that it might get better. Pappy was a biker, an Indian rider, a member of the "MC Rapid City", and also a "do-it" kind of guy.

It all started in 1936, and World War II was still far from being an issue, when Pappy and his friends made plans. They wanted to race somewhere off the street, preferably in such a way that they did not run the risk of getting tickets from the sheriff. For the hot-blooded young men, the city didn't give them anywhere where they could let off steam. The only problem was that they had no racetrack to vent their unbridled urge for speed.

Or did it?

At the fairground, in Sturgis, right in front of their faces, there was an old half-mile oval race track. This old racetrack was overgrown with bushes and weeds since it had not been used since the motorsport boom of the early 1900s.

That was the perfect solution for the young man ...

The boys went to work to make this racetrack as fast as possible again. It was not an easy task, because the money was tight, the "Rapid City Biker" had little money, and the Chamber of Commerce did not want to give them any grant. But somehow they mastered the work before the first snow fell and winter set in. The following year, they decided to market their idea by planning to make it an annual event called the grand "Black Hills Motor Classic". The proper application went through less than 12 months later, for which they also received the acknowledgement from the sport's umbrella organization, the American Motorcycle Association. The "Black Hills Motor Classic" got an official AMA approval for the 1938 planned half-mile race. The "MC Rapid City Motorcyclists" was then quickly renamed "The Jackpine Gypsies MC", and invited biker friends of the AMA Club to the summer races. To make the meeting even more attractive, a formal city parade with a band and various food booths were set up. That was the cornerstone for the biggest motorcycle rally in the world.

But in the beginning, not everything went well. After only a few years, as the Black Hills Classic was slowly becoming known, the Japanese bombed Pearl Harbor in December 1941. As a result, there was a rationing of fuel and so the rally had to take a break for the next two years. But, as the old saying goes, you cannot hold a wild horse or a good man - or in this case men!

With unbridled will, the "gypsies" were back and working harder than before to ensure the lasting success of their project. Of course, everything was fine and tidy then. The Sturgis-based bikers took their race seriously even after the Hollister incidents that had occurred in recent years, and the Harley riders were since then regarded as more of a kind of aggressive rabble. At Sturgis, everything was still very well-ordered, orderly and decent, on and off the track. At that time, in 1954, wild and unrestrained street behavior and wet T-shirt contests were still pretty much unknown, despite the classic "The Wild One". It was not like California, where back in the fifties and sixties there were problems with biker hooligans. This was Sturgis, South Dakota, a respectable small town. They had accepted an occasional influx of "motorcycle-crazy boys" here, but they were basically respectable and did not accept spitting, cursing hitting on married women. Back then the biggest crowd-pullers, aside from the races and the rides, were the "best-dressed riders" and the "best turn-out from clubs" competitions, and that's a big difference to today's "going-ones" during the Bike Week.

Some wish for those times of the early fifties, when Sturgis was still a relatively small, sociable affair. It was a gathering of a manageable number of people who valued elegance rather than alcohol. But time goes on and has it`s own dynamics. And as Daytona bikers became more and more annoyed and had problems with the Daytona police, they gradually moved north to Sturgis. They were looking for something less form a land more casual and unreserved, but that was not in the spirit of the founding fathers of the Sturgis Rally. More and more bikers came to Sturgis and this worried the organizers. There were soon many more bikers in the city than there were inhabitants, and so there was also more often problems with the police.

Between the parties, it escalated more and more and the bikers began to get more tickets. Motorcycles that were parked incorrectly were towed, people were arrested and campsites were burned before the event. The whole situation began to overheat, until at last, the tempers calmed down again and they found a common consensus.

The authorities began accepting the changes for purely economic reasons. In the late 1970s, more than 25,000 bikers appeared in the Black Hills, and five years later, the crowds of people had grown so much that the national parks, which were previously popular campsites, were declared prohibited areas to protect the protected and sensitive animals. Private campgrounds thrived overnight and provided the weary travelers with a place to stay in someone's front yard or behind a house, as there were simply not enough hotel and motel accommodations in the small town of about 7,000 inhabitants.

It's a challenge, but it's always well-managed, despite the sultry situations that come with a big event like this. The Bike Week has always been relatively trouble-free during the last few decades, and in spite of the potential danger due to increasing crowds, it never came to a catastrophe of any sort. The for-bearance of the indigenous people of the Black Hills, given what the annual invasion of a massive army of bikers and an 8-day occupation of strangers entails, is truly remarkable, not to mention the fact that during this time more money is spent than in the remaining weeks of the year all put together. That's why South Dakotans love the Americans bikes as well as those from overseas, and really sees them as a blessing on two wheels.

The attitude of the police department reflects the goings-on at the Bike Week as well. They do not take a break just because the "circus" is in town. Still, they are reserved and hold back a lot and behave remarkably restrained with regard to the politically sensitive nature of the event. Two days before the start of the rally, the Rapid City Journal once published a report titled "LAWMEN BRACE FOR PROBLEM" stating the words of US Marshall Gene A.: Alco-hol, gas, drugs and pistols:
This combination leads to possible difficulties in my opinion ... It has been going on for years - the rivalry between different clubs and gangs, and if you put them all together, they are a powder keg for potential difficulties.
Because the combination of gambling, drinking, drugs, weapons and the pos-sibility of illegal racing is the potential for the real problem – traffic accidents.

The Federal Police are always bothered by the Bike Week.
They do not like the bustle and the bikers, and they do not like the fact that the local police are not able to handle the event on their own and always need support again from them, as they are the better-equipped authority.
In addition, the field offices must be staffed by their own federal officials - the US Marshall Service, the Federal Bureau of Investigations, the Drug Enforce-ment Administration and the Alcohol, Tobacco and Gun Administration. They always have their hands full during this time and are pulled in to do things they would not have to do if it weren't for this Bike Week.

The politicians believe however, that everyone just wants to have a good time, and for that reason, they also believe that the crowd, with their basic momentum over the last few years, is managing itself quite well, which by and large makes them right.

The city administration is looking forward to this annual event as much as the bikers. The majority of people who visit the Motor Classic see it in the same way, because they respect the law and try to share the good feeling with the other rally visitors ...

"We have everything under control." is what they propagate year after year. People will feel safe here, have a great time and not have to worry.

Sturgis has become a trademark and is full of commercial success. How could it be otherwise, with all the good-humored, unreserved visitors, some of whom flock from far and wide into the city, and – regardless of what it costs - they would like to have a cool and relaxed break before they swing back on their bikes and glide into the sunset! But the Bike Week is also the proof that this is not just about a very profitable party for the organizers - it is also positive proof that brave citizens and bikers get along well for at least a week and accept each other so that there are no unnecessary escalating conflicts. It is a homage to the men and women who have given everything to build a legend - a legend called STURGIS!

Fads come and go, but Sturgis is getting bigger, more important and more popular, and/or it remains what it is - a legend!

Before this event, Sturgis was a totally sleepy village, a dullsville, but the rally turned it into a party in the northern Midwest, an oasis of the Harley Cult, a festival where bikers and their American motorcycles celebrate.

Alcohol may still be drunk only in the bars.

One still likes to remember the wild 70sin which the actual myth of "STURGIS" was created.

These times are long gone, but the stories of that time are the elixir, which gives the event the mystical attraction until today...

Motels far and wide are occupied at higher prices, and even at the campgrounds, there is hardly any room for the approaching hordes of motorcycle riders, and in the campground of the "Buffalo Chip" it is the most vehement ...

I've never seen such a mass flow of Harleys ever since. At Mount Rushmore, there was even a private parking lot and driveway for the bikers. So it is not only in Sturgis where the happenings are going on, but also in the surrounding towns and communities, and everywhere you see the same picture: the road-sides fully-parked with bikes, and there are really the most rustic people on the road. In the evening, there are parties that are pretty hard, at least for US standards. To get to Sturgis itself, you don't think you can get there by care because of the missing parking spaces, so you're best off coming by bike.

At the campgrounds outside of the city, where the long arm of the law does not go, completely different rules of the game apply "Show US YOUR TITS" This is a clear message, and a positive echo is usually guaranteed.
Here is not the place where moral apostles and priests would feel comfortable, certainly not here, because here you do what you like, and if possible, com-pletely unrestrained. Everyone here worships the only one God who gives them the opportunity to go outside of society to pay homage to their own val-ues, if they believe in anything ...
This God has two cylinders, and in his veins "gasoline and oil" flow!

Quelle: https://commons.wikimedia.org/wiki/File:Flag_of_South_Dakota.svg, „Flag of South Dakota", Lizenz: https://creativecommons.org/licenses/by-sa/3.0/legalcode

Hundreds of thousands let themselves be seen and celebrate during the Bike Week

... also the Veteran's club is actively involved…

See and be seen is the name of the game …

The air is full with gasoline and thunder ...

... because the pipes of the engines set the pace.

There is almost nothing that does not exist here ...

The temperatures are about 25°C (77°F), which, for the Bike Week, is usually mild. Usually it is about 35°C (95°F) or more at this time ...

Outlines that inspire…

One of the bikes is leaking gas; the "cops" check out what's going on ...
or to see if it's something more relevant ... everything's easy-going!

Helmets are rarely seen here, and the exhaust pipes are open ...

Minor repairs are done on the spot ...

If a helmet, then something very unique ...

What more do you need…?!

… good-humored and chilling-out types ... what else ... ?!

Grilled specialties entice ...

... crazy bikes on every corner ...

USA, the land…

… the almost unlimited possibilities!

No Limit… just…

…wild, wild West!

... and everything always prickling ...!

… and should be nice and colorful… !

Also, many women like to firmly turn the gas tap ...

…or let it be turned!

... the cops are really nice here and let the good game run its course...

... and relax even on the weirdest bikes ...

... on a family trip ...!

It's like a magnet that just attracts everything...!

... off to Main Street, ... to the party ...!

Wearing sunglasses when riding a bike is mandatory in South Dakota!

Shots from a little further away from the center of town...

... barely a moment without the thunderous sound of a V-Twin ...!

Riding, riding, riding… world of gasoline and thunder…!

… and cool and crazy T-shirts in heaps ...

The man of the right faith is also at the fore front ...

The whole thing here is an almost thoroughly polished affair ...

The man with the knotted beard wanted him and his cool purple bike to be eternalized in my book ...!

... the "Cops" are only marginal figures here and are brought in for the Bike Week from the whole country. Before and after this event, this town with its approximately 7000 inhabitants is extremely quiet. The shops earn their money at this time, and they can live well from it for the rest of the year.

Everyone joins in

…and have fun…!

The really wild years (70s and 80s) are over. At that time, hardcore bikers also liked to pile up Japs machines and light them on fire on the spot ...!

He is the right guy… because he's maybe a priest or something similar…:-P

... whether on two or three wheels ... they all roll/glide all ... quite relaxed ...

…pleasure…

… and joy!

Sturgis – What is it?

In the contemplative town of 7000 souls, the largest Harley-Davidson festival in the world is rising.

Far and wide, you hardly see a trace of Asian or British bikes - in Sturgis in early August Harley Davidson reigns!

At the beginning of August, around 420,000 followers of freedom on two wheels met there for the 77th time to party, flaunt and sniff gas and exhaust! Most of the bikers come from the USA, of course, but also Harley-madmen from South America and even Europe are embarking on the long journey from August 4th-12th to indulge in their passion.

Bizarre Rituals

Aside from the fact that in Sturgis there was hardly a patch of space available, and some locals rented their front gardens as tent sites, the tattooed and full-bearded guys made for a not too excessive spectacle. They caroused themselves and their steel fire-starters in a frenzy of acceleration races at the traffic lights and intersections on the outskirts of town. What began in the daytime on the streets and saloons was lived out after sunset, not only by masses of alcohol or rowdiness. Here you could leave the everyday life far behind and do what you only dreamed of all year long. The whole atmosphere was filled with crackling freedom and was full of electricity from the enthusiastic gathering of like-minded people, for whom their bike is a kind of fulfillment worth living for ... Ride to live and live to ride ...!

Attract Attention at Any Price

Tattoos, piercings, loud machines: all this is the order of the day at the Harley-Davidson gathering. Anyone who wants to attract attention (and many want it) must be especially creative - or exhibitionistic! So also the - let's say discreetly corpulent - ladies in net tops, which show more than they cover. Other fans of naked skin present themselves in a touch of nothing or transparent negligees. But if that's not enough, you can get your blood pressure pumping between "real men" at the wet T-Shirt contest or the Women's Mud Catfight. There is also a so-called "midget bowling", where dwarfs or small people are used/abused as a kind of bowling ball to overturn bowling pins. In addition to bizarre rituals and a lot of bare skin, the bikes are sometimes ridden - the area around Sturgis, especially in the Black Hills is really magnificent!

Sturgis and Surroundings is Considered a True Biker's Paradise
Fortunately, the flashing fire chairs are not only put on display, but also ridden out. Around Sturgis there are beautiful roads in the middle of the Badlands National Park with absolutely breathtaking landscapes. In less than an hour you can reach Mount Rushmore, Iron Mountain Road, Custer State Park, Needle's Highway, Spearfish Canyon or marvel at the wild buffalo herds along the roads - and unlike Route 66, there are many curves here!

Above all, this is also a living legend and not just a myth like the "66", which, since 1974, has largely lost its reason for existing through a new interstate. It has now degenerated to a tourist attraction with a very poor road surface in many places.

No, if you're going to go on a US Highway, then travel on one that is not a dead myth but a living legend - STURGIS is alive, and it's pulsing with life ...! ☺

More and more bikers are coming to town ...

From 18 to 88 years, everything is in...

… bright metal with its inherent power and shapely erotic ...

… the streets are filling up …

… it attracts more and more party people …!

Extroverted types are completely at home here!

Cool women and their fat machines ...

It's best to chill for a while in the shade!

... hot treats wherever you look ...

Simply good…

… music, beer and everywhere the dull burbling of engines …!

Family Restaurant, …and also elegant with his yellow cylinder …!

Lovely…

... and old machines ... (HD from 1922)!

The stream of riders who push into the city does not stop ...

... instead is steadily growing ...!

Only from above you can get an overview!

More…, and moooore …

…and fun without end!

Neil, Liz and John …!

Oldy… but goldy!

Towards evening, the party increasingly shifts to the bars and makeshift saloons - because no alcohol may be drunk on the street. Riots and excesses are rare, Officer Luke W. is calm. In any case, in earlier days, much more had been going on, Sturgis veteran Carlos M. looks back. In particular, an incident from the rowdy 70s, when rock bands invaded the town and parked and torched Japanese motorcycles in the middle of the park, has burned into his memories: A bunch of drunks had dumped gasoline over the four-lane road, then rode full throttle with their Harleys to break through the wall of fire - the drivers were naked and most were almost completely drunk or lost their inhibitions due to other drugs and were ready for anything. Bikers live extremely, ... at least in the hardcore variant ...☺

These are the stories that made Sturgis a legend - and ultimately ensure good business for the locals. Somehow everyone seems to benefit, there is hardly one for whom a piece of the cake does not fall off: Along the Main Street, which is trafficked by busy two-wheelers all day long, children sell cool drinks. Lightly-dressed girls offer motorcycle care in a bikini. Not only front gardens are converted into parking spots and campsites. Almost every inhabitant of the city takes part is one way or another.

Some are completely devoted to the myth of Sturgis. Like Carlos M., who quit his art galleries and entered the business of selling T-shirts and accessories. Today he has several stores and a thriving Internet trade. He always stayed in Sturgis and has not missed a single rally. If you ask him if he has made it to being a rich man, he smiles and says, "I work four months a year and can live the other eight pretty well."

Here is it all as if we were inebriated, all that really matters is to let it go unbridled ... and let it go really well ...☺

The bar in the basement is an insider tip

Birthday party in the Dungeon Bar…!

…she just said he should not say anything to her father ...

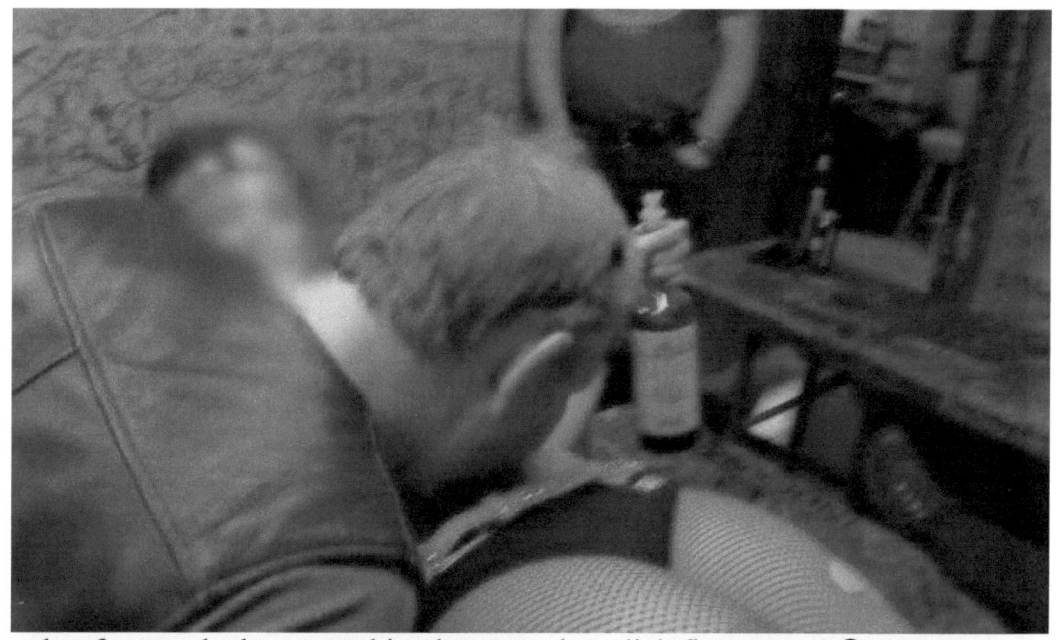

…but for now he has something better to do ... lick fine cream! ☺

Underground Sturgis…! ☺

Hell broke loose in the Knuckle Saloon!

Simply good … whether mature or…

… young … it makes absolutely no difference…

a real bone shaker! ☺

No matter where you look ...

... noble frenzy and pure enjoyment ...!

Crossing roads is not always easy at this time ...

V8 Boss Hoss machines with around 450 hp

Here are some interesting facts about South Dakota:

- Gasoline prices are about 50 Eurocents/liter.
- Electricity prices are at about 7 Eurocents/kWh (In Germany, about 30 Eurocents).
- On the highways, one is sometimes completely alone over longer distances, which is not entirely safe in the event of a breakdown or accident.
- The movie "Dances with Wolves" was filmed south of Rapid City.
- The people here in SD are very open, friendly and almost everyone has the desire and time for non-binding small talk.

Voluptuous machines ... and relaxed and satisfied riders ...!

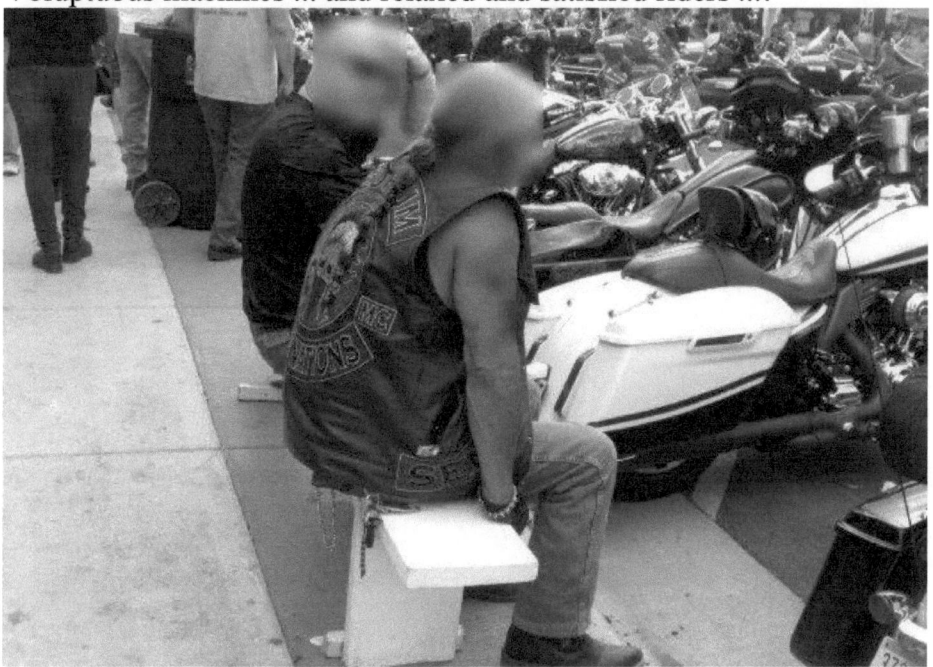

…you have to taste the awesome atmosphere…! ☺

Steel steeds… wherever you look…!

… crazy bars and nice girls …!

Main Street Sturgis … Is there anything more beautiful…?!!

In the meantime you can see Japanese motorcycles like these from time to time, technically perfect Suzuki VS1400 or others from the Nippon country.

STURGIS, love it or leave it…!   Nooo, you`ll looove it !!! !!! !!!

The Bike Weeks at the end of the 60s and 70s were pretty rough and wild, but that's lightly increased in the 80s ...

In the 1980s, there were more and more major clashes between warring MCs, which sometimes led to major gang wars, and the "fights" were staged on the streets of Sturgis.

What we experienced here in 2017 was not yet completely family-friendly and really for youths, but the really wild years with dozens of deaths due to violent clashes or traffic accidents due to illegal races (some done on absolutely un-rideable roads) are fortunately long ago past.

Visitor Numbers of the "STURGIS Rally" Over the Last Decades

Year	No. Visitors	Comment
1938	175	first rally, Jackpine Gypsies
1939	300	
1940	450	
1941	500	
1942	- -	No rally due to gas rationing during WW II
1943	- -	No rally due to gas rationing during WW II
1944	650	
1950	1000	
1960	2.500	
1970	7.000	
1978	25.000	
1980	35.000	
1985	150.000	
1990	400.000	50-year anniversary
2000	600.000	
2005	525.000	
2010	460.000	
2015	750.000	75-year anniversary
2016	400.000	
2017	420.000	

…no comment needed! ☺

Bike wash for only 30.- Box (Dollar)

Beauties made of steel…!

Evening, on the way to the Buffalo Chip Campground ...!

...and again and again you see bikes that are loaded "really good" ...

... and here again a pure feast for the eyes !!

…everyone is in a good mood!

Authentic and incredible ...

... because real beauty comes only from the inside ...!

... and quick to hit in the highest gears ...!

The views are great ... from above as well as below ...!

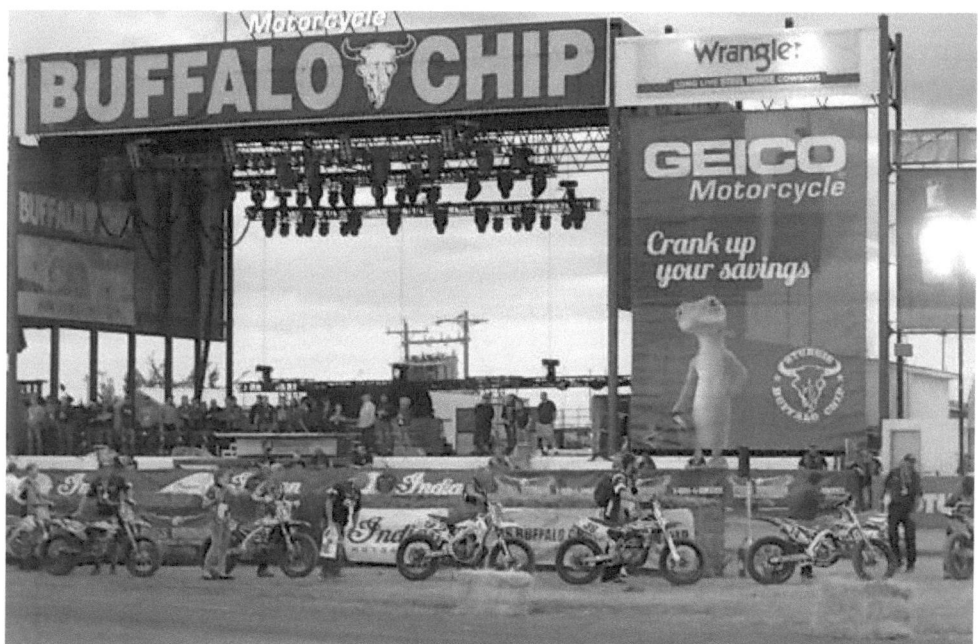

First the Rallye…

… and …

... then the Buffalo chip stage was rebuilt...

... and the SHINEDOWN concert followed!

Bikers come to Sturgis and the Buffalo Chip from all parts of the USA.
Also many are from overseas like Europe and Australia ...

7.08.2017(Monday)

The day after the big party at the Buffalo Chip, our program included riding to Mount Rushmore, Custer State Park, and on Iron Mountain Road, Needles Highway, on to Crazy Horse and back to Deadwood!

Quelle: https://commons.wikimedia.org/wiki/File:Mount_Rushmore.jpg,
Lizenz: Public Domain

Extrem kurviger Abschnitt auf der Iron Mountain Road…

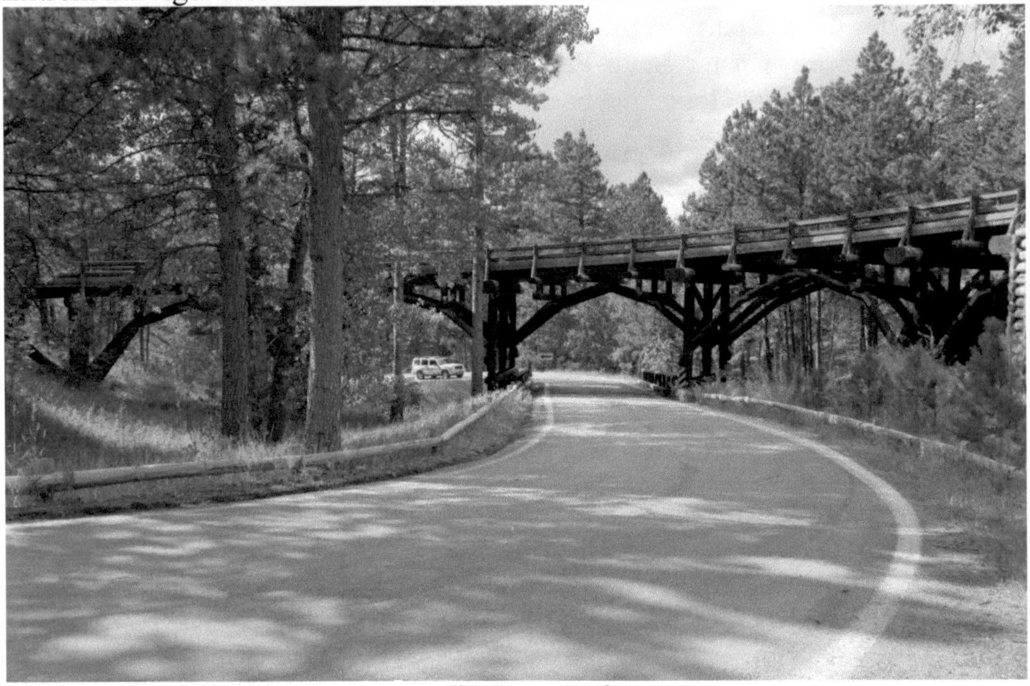

Quelle: KimonBerlin, https://commons.wikimedia.org/wiki/File:Pigtail_bridge_(328815220).jpg, „Pigtail bridge (328815220)", Lizenz: https://creativecommons.org/licenses/by-sa/2.0/legalcode

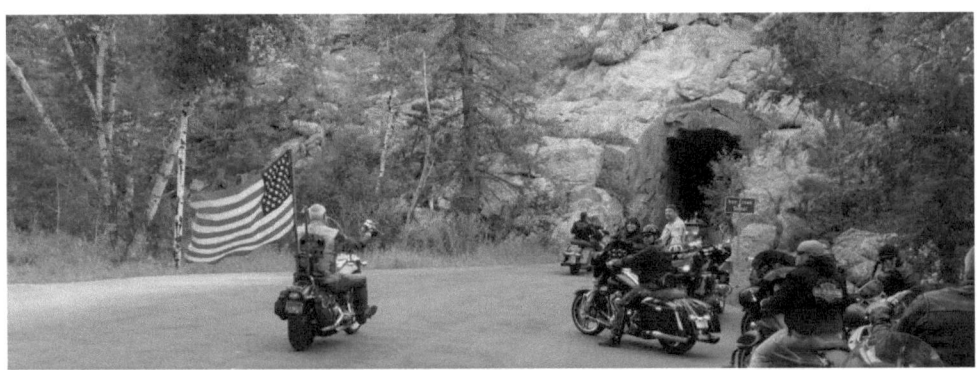

... and again and again traffic jams to get through the narrow tunnels ...☺

Impressive rock formations that really only exist here ...

Stop and go, because some tunnels can only be ridden through one at a time!

Nature pur...!

A place to rest and unwind ...

Crazy Horse Monument…

…a most likely eternally-driven construction site of a sculpture of a great Indian!

Deadwood, a paradise for biker…

…and gamblers.

08.08.2017(Tuesday)
Breakfast, packing, cleaning up the cabin, and start the return trip to Howard (356 miles/570km). John hast to be back to the University on August 8th.

„Goodbye" …to the cabin…

… and the wild game, which is already almost within reach.

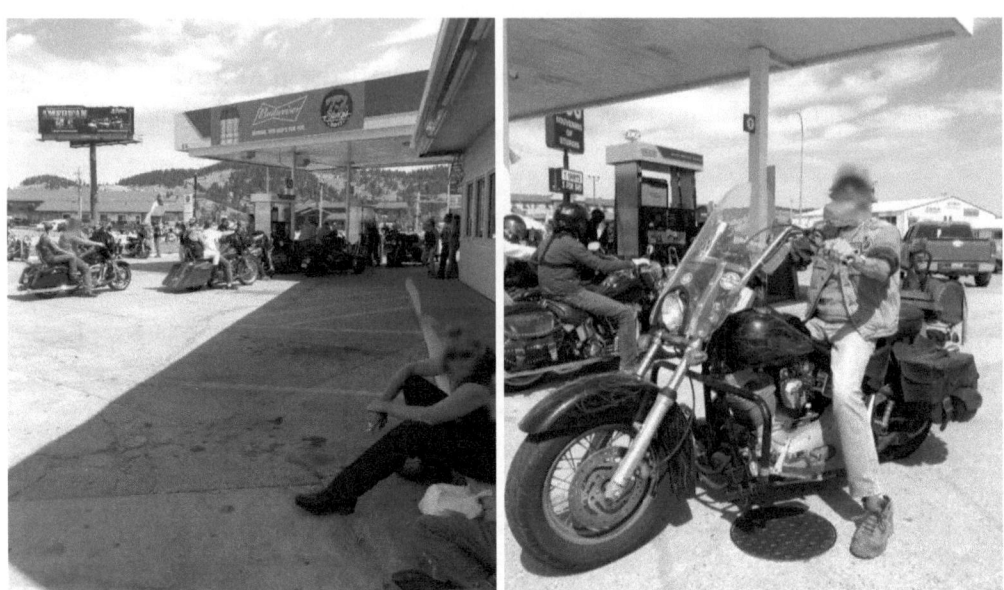

…Motorcycle traffic jam at a gas station in Sturgis …!
After refueling the bikes, it's out of the party zone and back onto Highway34, back to the East …

Discovered a cool machine at a gas station, which just had to go into the book!

…endless Highway-34, … much further than the eye can see …!

After about 130 miles (210km), and driving through an almost completely unspoiled prairie, we had our first stop at a gas station called T34, which had a small and simple restaurant.

... some biker refueling after a long ride ...!

... parked motorcycles in front of T34 ...

back at Pierre, crossing over the Missouri River from West River to East River

Mac`s Corner, a store and gas station somewhere on Highway34 between Pierre and Fort Thompson. The shop guy has been working there for over 60 years and always has a friendly smile on his face ...

Mailbox collection point behind "Mac`s-Corner" for the farmers which live in the area and where the way to get to them is too far for the postman. Located on Highway 34 between Sturgis and Howard, somewhere in the "middle of nowhere"!

(Mac`s C. is on the edge of an Indian reservation through which we drove)

… back in the same motel in Howard as a week ago!

…Water tower and gas station on at the entrance of town, on Highway 34…

09.08.2017(Wednesday)

After returning to Howard, it's time to rest and have an extensive breakfast. Buy beef jerky, wash clothes, prepare pictures for the book, and in the evening, go to brother Jerry's to shoot with him.

One of the recreational sports in South Dakota ... sharp shooting!

Jerry Winker owns some very interesting, as well as rare, firearms of all calibers and makes some of his own ammunition. It is quite normal to shoot several times a week and to practice one's right to self-defense. People here don't know it any differently, and there would be something missing if it were not so. Freedom and personal fulfillment are still very important here, of course, only as long as you leave your neighbor in peace ...! (Jerry is an official shooting coach, by the way.)

Shooting exercises with an AR-15 behind the farmhouse.

In South Dakota, you start shooting sharp weapons when you are about 10-12 years old, which is about the same age as when you learn to drive a car in the countryside. Starting with 14, you can officially drive in the company of an adult driver. However, if you do not have an adult with you or you are under 14 years of age and you get caught, in the worst case, you will get a warning or a ticket for a few dollars from the sheriff or deputy.

Here you can see everything a little more relaxed and can "leave the church in the village" (a German saying).

A saying in South Dakota: **"Give me a gun and leave me alone!"**
  ... or: **"Let it go with the flow ...!"** ☺

(PS: The girl in the photo was not allowed to shoot the weapon, but got permission to hold an unloaded one explicitly for this picture.)

10.08.2017(Thursday)
Visit to the Corn Palace in Mitchell and the village museum in Howard, worked on the book, and in the evening, we grilled some big and hearty Angussteaks with John and Liz's Mom, and enjoyed them with some spicy American Barbeque sauce.

Corn Palace in Mitchell

1904 WORLD FAMOUS

With Mitchell competing to be the state capital, exposition organizers voted to hire the world-famous John Phillip Sousa Band. To the astonishment of his manager, Mitchell agreed to pay $7,000 for six days. When Sousa arrived and saw Mitchell's dirt streets, he refused to let his musicians leave the train until he received payment in full. Bankers countered by bringing the total in cash to the depot. Sousa gave three concerts daily rather than the prearranged two. National attention guaranteed the continuation of the festival, though Pierre won the bid for the capital.

1907 GOOD FORTUNE

The "swastika" symbol on the 1907 palace was an Indian motif, dating back thousands of years and representing prosperity, peace and good fortune. John Phillip Sousa and his famous band returned to enthusiastic crowds.

It is interesting that the swastika is not only an Indo-European symbol, but also a very old Native American symbol for prosperity, peace and a good future. The Nazis did not invent this symbol but abused it shamelessly for their own purposes ...☹

One of the first things I noticed in the museum ...

... loot from Germany in a small village in South Dakota:
Swastika flag, 0815 machine gun and carbine made by the company Mauser

Snap-

-shots

…taken on a rural road near Howard (Fedora) ...

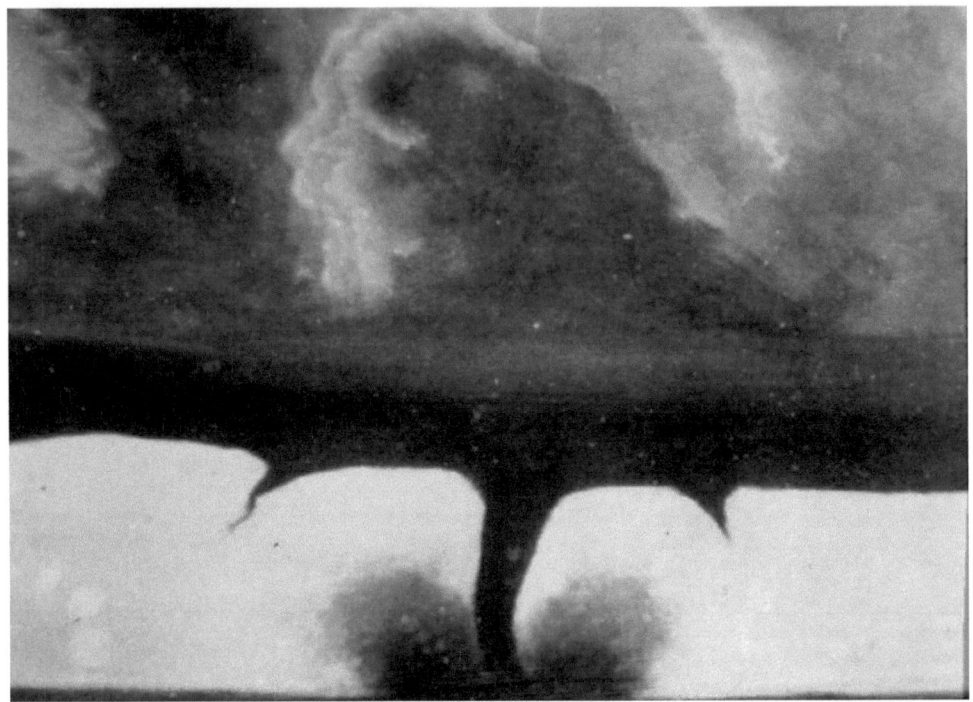

..and again something interesting ...!
This is the first photo ever taken of a tornado on August 28, 1884, in Howard, South Dakota.
There are coincidences ...

South Dakota is a wild country with some Indian reservations.
A few years ago, they wanted to introduce vehicle inspections, but after a relatively short time, they gave up because they were rejected by the inhabitants because of the high costs ("unnecessary" repairs). There is so little happening on the highways that it is kind of justifiable in its own way...
As I said, the love of freedom is still ranked highest here,
and what does not necessarily have to be done, won't be done ...☺

About 15 years ago, there was an action called "Clean Up South Dakota". As part of this initiative, it was possible to burn down old dilapidated barns that you no longer needed, including anything in them, under the supervision of the local fire department. The ashes were then buried with the help of a bulldozer in a large hole next to where the fire was lit. Environmental protection was and is still is not written very "big" here. As I said, it is still a bit "wild, wild west" here ...!

Original photo of an old barn, which was disposed of on the Winker premises in this way!

…and on the way every now and then a few snap shots…

…you better use snake stopper around your house here…!

11.08.2017(Friday)

Return to St. Paul via Granite Falls. Visit to the Indian quarry in Pipestone and a World War II museum, followed by of burgers and a good malt beer at the Native American-ran casino

Soft stone pipe heads from the quarry in Pipestone ...

…which is now under Native American administration and is considered cultural property!

Rock face in Pipestone

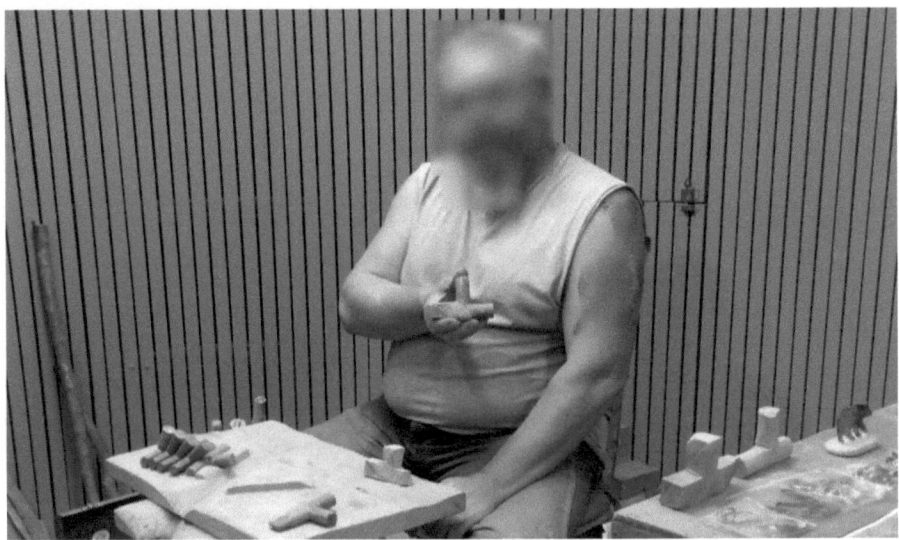

Pipe maker in Pipestone (Half Native American)

Landscape in the Pipestone quarry...

... The famous Native American peace pipes are made from this relatively soft rock.

Impressions from Granite Falls…

Museum with German Messerschmidt B109 ... (rare WW II airplane)

…then delicious food in the casino ...

... then enjoy the sunset while leaning on the '68 Ford Falcon!

12.08.2017(Saturday)
Drive from Granite Falls back to Minneapolis to John's place.
Rest, relax and continue writing on the manuscript for the book

A 1957 Bel Air, about 40,000 Miles for $ 60,000, seen at a car dealer about one hour west of Minneapolis …

13.08.2017 (Sunday)

Closing dinner on the next-to-last evening before the return flight to Frankfurt

14.08.2017(Monday)

 Visit downtown Minneapolis, which is adjacent to St. Paul. The two cities are therefore also called Twin-Cities ...

…downtown Minneapolis…

Parking Rates

Calculated From 5:00am - 4:59am
Rates Include All Taxes
For Assistance Call: 612-305-2119

0 - 20 Mins	
21 - 40 Mins	$ 8.00
41 - 60 Mins	$10.00
61 - 80 Mins	$12.00
81 - 100 Mins	$14.00
101 - 120 Mins	$16.00
121 - 180 Mins	$18.00
3 - 6 Hours	$20.00
6 - 10 Hours	$21.00
10 Hours - End of Day	$22.00
	$23.00

Parking fees in Minneapolis…

… ALDIs have been around for a few years in St. Paul/Minneapolis

On this Monday evening, we packed and in the evening, got a visit from John's brother Dan and his wife Karin.

For the farewell dinner, I then did my best "crazy cooking skills" and cobbled together some hearty burgers, which had a lot of garlic, onion, pepper, chili and parsley.

Of the "German Burgers", not a single one remained ...

As soon as the beer was drunk and the visit passed away, we went to bed a little earlier than usual, because the next day we would be going to the airport and back home over the big pond ...☺

15.08.2017(Tuesday)
The return flight from Minneapolis to Chicago was around noon, and from there, we flew with a Boeing 747 back to Germany.

16.08.2017(Wednesday)
Arrival at Frankfurt airport and return to Karlsruhe ... ☺
The jet lag from flying east, meaning from the USA to Europe, hit us harder and us firmly under its control. The next few days, we will have a bit of a fight with that, but that does not matter, because the trip was without exception cool and impressive!

THE END

For those of you who want to get more information and want to play with the idea of going to Sturgis for yourself, I have added some important information here that could be very useful.

For example, there is a guide in English dealing with the Black Hills area. The book is an absolute "MUST" for all bikers who want to know the area a bit better ...☺

This book **„Black Hills Motorcycle Rides"**
(author: Paul Michel, price 10$) can be ordered at the following address:

- **www.blackhillsparks.org/books**
- **Tel.: 001-605-745-7020 (USA)**
- **E-Mail: bhpf@blackhillsparks.org**

Links to the best sightseeing points in South Dakota!

http://highwayhighlights.com/2013/04/reconciliation-park-mankato-mn/

http://walnutgrove.org/museum.html

https://www.nps.gov/pipe/index.htm

http://visitbrookingssd.com/

http://www.desmetsd.com/desmet/visitors/laura-ingalls-wilder

http://www.cityofhoward.com/

http://www.cornpalace.org/

http://www.mitchellindianvillage.org/

http://www.plattesd.org/

https://en.wikipedia.org/wiki/White_River,_South_Dakota

https://www.tripadvisor.de/Tourism-g60729-Interior_South_Dakota-Vacations.html

http://www.blackhillsbadlands.com/scenic-drives/badlands-loop-state-scenic-byway

http://www.onlyinyourstate.com/south-dakota/scenic-abandoned-town-sd/

https://en.wikipedia.org/wiki/Wounded_Knee_Battlefield

http://www.walldrug.com/

https://www.visitrapidcity.com/

https://www.nps.gov/moru/index.htm

http://www.ironmountainroad.com/

https://custerresorts.com/activities/activities-in-the-park/

https://custerresorts.com/activities/scenic-drives/needles-highway/

https://custerresorts.com/activities/scenic-drives/peter/

https://custerresorts.com/activities/scenic-drives/wildlife-loop/

http://www.blackhillsbadlands.com/places/sylvan-lake

http://harneypeakinfo.com/

https://crazyhorsememorial.org/

https://www.1880train.com/

https://www.bearcountryusa.com/

http://www.blackhillsbadlands.com/drives/spearfish-canyon-scenic-byway

http://www.blackhillsbadlands.com/scenic-drives/boulder-canyon

http://www.blackhillsbadlands.com/scenic-drives/vanocker-canyon-nemo-road

http://www.blackhillsbadlands.com/parks-monuments/bear-butte-state-park

http://www.spiritualtravels.info/articles-2/north-america/bear-butte-in-south-dakota/

http://www.pactolalake.com/

http://www.blackhillsbadlands.com/parks-monuments/angostura-state-recreation-area

http://cosmosmysteryarea.com/index.html

http://www.reptilegardens.com/

https://www.nps.gov/wica/index.htm

http://www.wildmustangs.com/

https://prairieedge.com/

http://www.blackhillsbadlands.com/business/dinosaur-park

http://www.sdairandspacemuseum.com/

https://www.deadwood.com

https://www.nps.gov/deto/index.htm

http://mammothsite.com

http://www.sdsmt.edu/Academics/Museum-of-Geology/Home/

Reference Disclaimer

For direct or indirect references to other Internet sites ("links") lying outside of the responsibility of the editor, a liability would only be incurred if the publisher of the content was aware of false content and had taken technically possible and reasonable efforts to prevent the use of illegal content. The editor of the pages from the www.soundsofspirit.de site expressly declares that at the time of linking, the corresponding linked sites were free of illegal content. The publisher has no influence on the current and future design and content of the linked pages. Therefore, songsofspirit.de dissociates itself explicitly from all contents of all linked pages that are changed after the link. This applies to all links set within the site. For illegal, incorrect or incomplete content, and for damages resulting from the use or disuse of information, it is the provider of the site referred to who is responsible, and not the one who has linked to these pages.

Short report by John Winker about the trip to Sturgis!
(August 17 at 6:22am)
Now that life's back to "normal," I want to chronicle the past 3 weeks of life. Everything was pretty simple until the evening of July 26th when my sister Liz (Elizabeth Winker) and my friend Lou, flew into town from Germany. Liz was last home for Christina's graduation, and we started talking about heading to Sturgis. 16-months later, it was go-time. Liz & Lou flew from Germany to ride motorcycles to Sturgis, SD. And I was the guide. We spent the first few days tooling around St. Paul & Minneapolis, letting Lou get used to the Victory - the motorcycle we purchased specifically for this trip, but he had never ridden until now - and getting supplies in order to actually make it to Sturgis. We left St. Paul on July 31st, with the Valkyrie leading the pack, Lou following on the Victory, and Liz following in the Falcon - YES, the car I purchased back in March that didn't have rear spring perches until May. #Roadkill. And, yes, the recovery vehicle for this trip was the oldest and least-reliable vehicle of the team. We made it to Howard, SD that evening, said our hello's to Pat (aka, mom) and prepped for the real deal. We headed to Platte, SD on August 2rd and stayed with our Uncle Barney and wife Connie. She recently stopped riding, so she lent Liz her riding gear (incredibly fit perfect!) for the rest of the trip. Liz traded the Falcon for Jerry's Flex for this part of the trip, given the Falcon's lack of power steering, power brakes, . . . power . . . , and Air Conditioning (or heat, as we would later find out). August 3th, we headed west from Platte in a drizzly and cold mess. By the time we hit White River, SD, Lou was starting to question his decisions (me too), but by Interior, SD, things were clearing up. We fueled at Cowboy Corner at Interior, SD, and as we were leaving, Lou fired up the Victory to a round of attention and cheers from the crowd (the V92 is REALLY loud, but not like a Harley, it's distinctly different, and I think everybody recognized that). We headed for Wall through the Badlands. We stopped to take some awesome pictures of Liz playing her traditional Native American flute against some of the most brutal and beautiful landscape the world has to offer. #Wall Drug gave us enough nickel coffee and free ice water to keep going. Back through the Badlands, then onto Rapid City as dusk approached, we continued west as the temperatures dove south. Now, let me tell you something, dear reader, when I originally rented our cabin, Gold Run Cabin, I did not *REALIZE* it was part of Terry Peak, the world-renowned Black Hills Ski and Sky locale. Temps were diving into the upper 40's as we arrived at the cabin, and we were COLD. Lou fired up the wood stove, we cracked a beer, and considered what we had just accomplished. Lou had just set a new daily mileage record for himself, Liz had just gotten her awesome pictures in the

Badlands, and I had just taken our group across two states to get away from everything. It was a good end to a great day. The following five days were filled with motorcycles, music, mayhem, nature, exhaustion, beauty, construction, congestion, friendship, fellowship, and some of the best weather Sturgis Bike Week has ever offered. We were only rained-out one day in our entire tour (and we *could* have ridden, it just would've been stupid to do so). The purpose of this trip was to show Lou, a German citizen, what Sturgis Bike Rally is really all about. We rode the main roads, we visited the Buffalo Chip Campground, we watched the races, we saw a band (#Shinedown), and we saw 420,000 other bikers who shared the same aspirations. Lou met my family, my friends (Burghardt & Josh), and my padres who share this hobby here in the US. Lou is writing a book (in German) about the Sturgis Bike Rally experience. While we only spent a week, and we spent the week in a great cabin an hour away from Sturgis, these truths ring through. To say the trip was without incident would take away from the numerous *positive* incidents we saw. Granted, the Victory blew a low-beam lamp & the Valkyrie is getting some tail lamp wiring attention, but overall, nothing major went wrong - we were never stranded. In our extended group, my friend Josh went down avoiding a bus, but only minor scrapes and scratches, no broken bones. Most important to me, we watched the races at Buffalo Chip with my Uncle Dick & Marsha Wagner for the first time since I've started riding. Lou met Dick, Marsha, Connie, and Barney Jr. whom he would've otherwise missed, not to mention Barney Sr. & Connie in Platte. We headed out of Lead on August 8th, "cannonballing" it back to Howard, shattering Lou's daily mileage record. (I'm not sure, but I think we almost doubled it prior to this trip?) At one point, Lou might have verified the V92 has a top speed > 160kmh (that's 100mph, for the US friends) and I might have confirmed the Valk can still hit 180kmh (110mph) even after 96,000 miles. (Good thing we might have done this on roads that were neither Federal nor Indian Reservation somewhere nondescript in an area somewhere in South Dakota, not where either of us are living.) As far as I'm concerned, this confirmed Lou's status as part of our family, though I do want my sister to make sure we aren't previously related. Once back to Howard, we diverged. I headed back to the Cities on August 9th, another rainy and cold day. I followed the rain almost the entire trip back, but I had to since I had class on the weekend. Liz & Lou met up on Saturday, August 12. They spent a few extra days in Howard, then made their way to St. Paul via Granite Falls with the Victory & Falcon again. We spent the weekend pretty low-key, putting very few miles on the bikes, and not many more on the Falcon. We spent most of the time coordinating our pictures, videos and stories. Liz & Lou hit the airport on 8/15, and I just got word from her they made it to Germany without incident. The great, international Sturgis vacation is done. Well . . . the FIRST great international Sturgis vacation is done. There may be more.

WOW...

... and now I want to say a very big THANKS to the general manager of this gorgeous trip... !

John is a real smart and nice guy. He`s always happy and in a good shape...!

A VERY BIG THANKS FOR ALL TO MY AMERICAN FRIEND MR. JOHN WINKER AND HIS VERY INTERSTING AND NICE FAMILY!!!

With the best wishes your friend Lou (Lothar R. Schulz)

Hi everyone,

I have a short but important info that is great in itself!... ☺

If you want to really deeply relax, then go to the homepage of Elizabeth Winker (Liz) .

She has been playing various Native American (Style) flutes for over 10 years, and she is really good at it. Especially beautiful and impressive, I find the Native American (Style) Love flute especially impressive. It really goes under the skin ...!

By the way, she was also on the trip to Sturgis ...

She grew up in Winfred, South Dakota, and, according to family ancestry research, has most likely a bit of Native American in her ancestry (Sioux or Cheyenne) ...

The spiritual spirit, which is not only present in her music, has something especially deep, fresh ..., very positive and relaxed ...!

A title of hers is for example: Hangin` out at a Desert Gas Station ...!

Songs of Spirit
Music of the Native American Style Flute

by Elizabeth Winker

In today's fast-paced world where we are often confronted with tight schedules, change and stress, the soothing and healing tones of the Native American (Style) Flute can help restore inner peace and harmony. They can open the hearts of those who play, as well as those who listen, returning each to his or her own inner Source, and can each to get a chance to experience the wonder of unconditional love.

Check it out, ... you`ll be surprised...!!! ☺